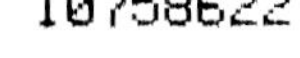

THIS COLORING BOOK BELONGS TO

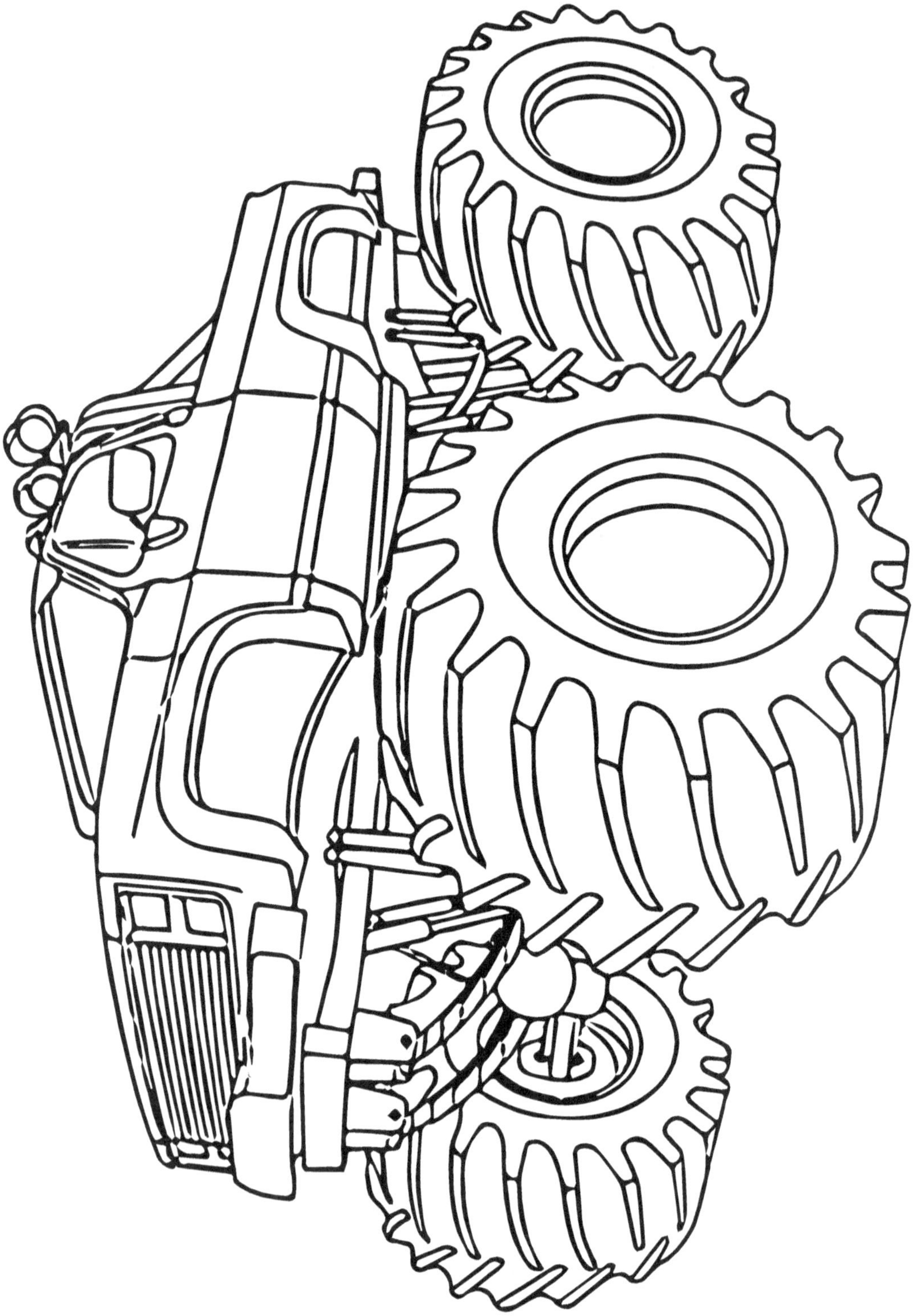

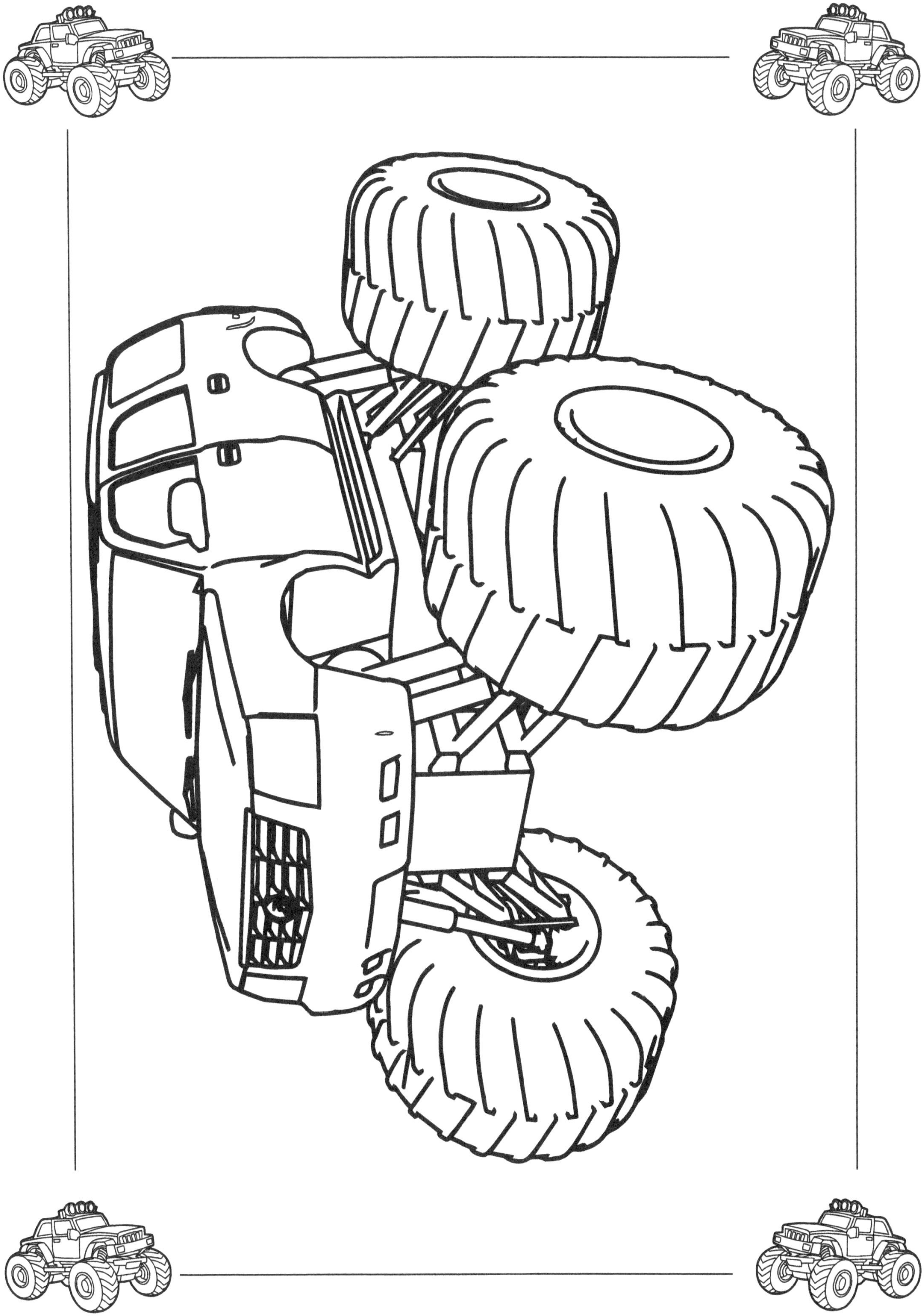

HELP THE MONSTRE

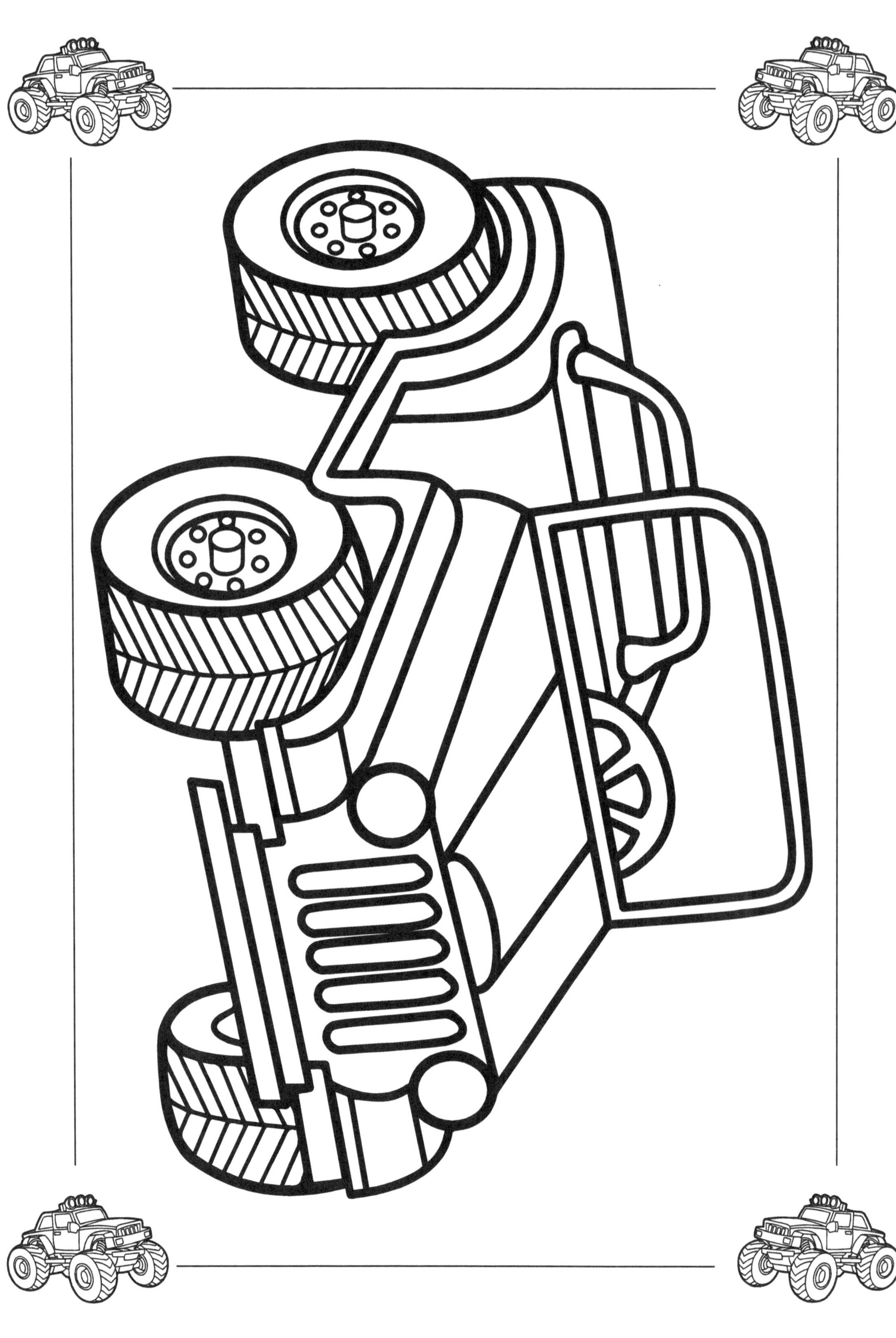

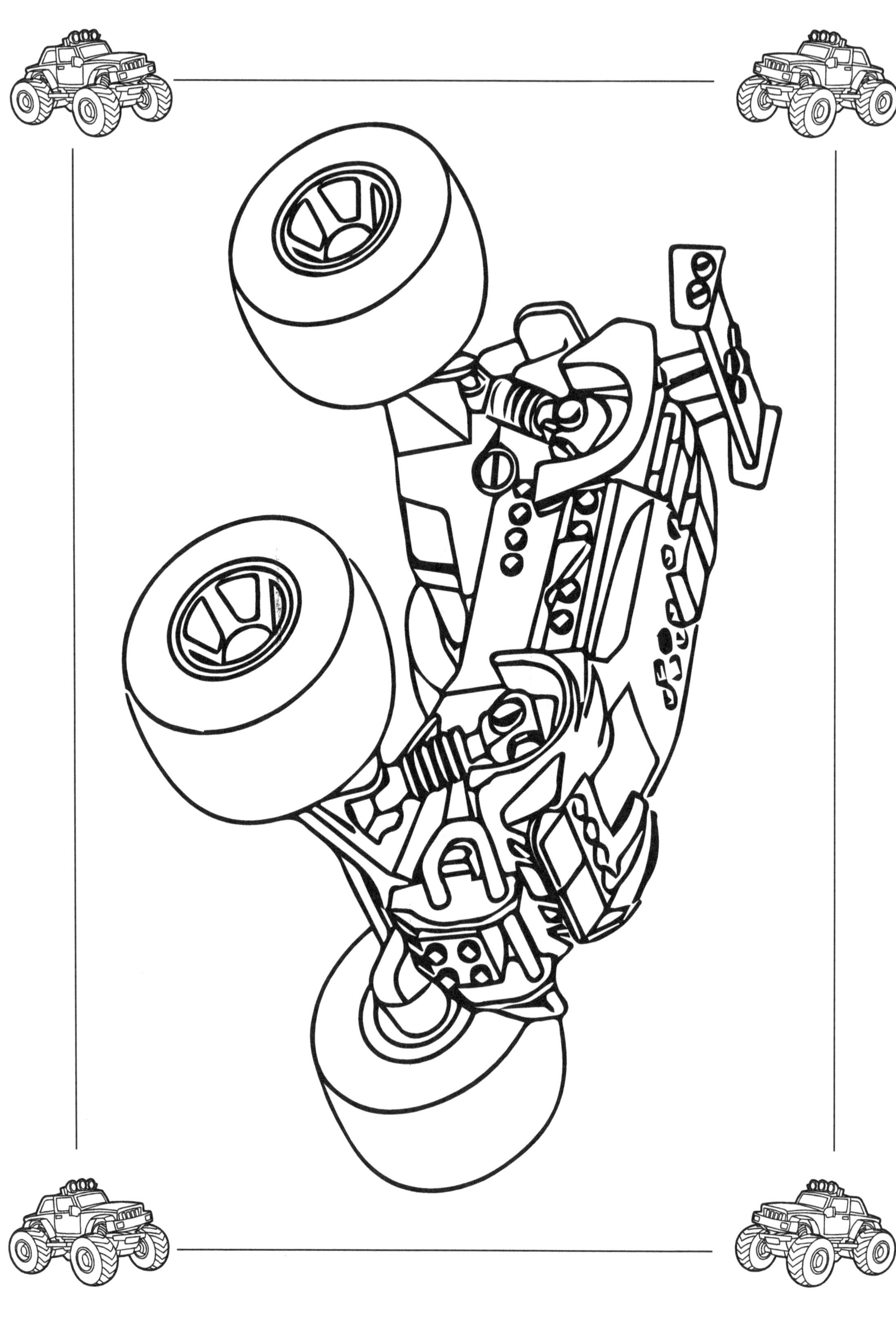

FEED THE MONSTRE

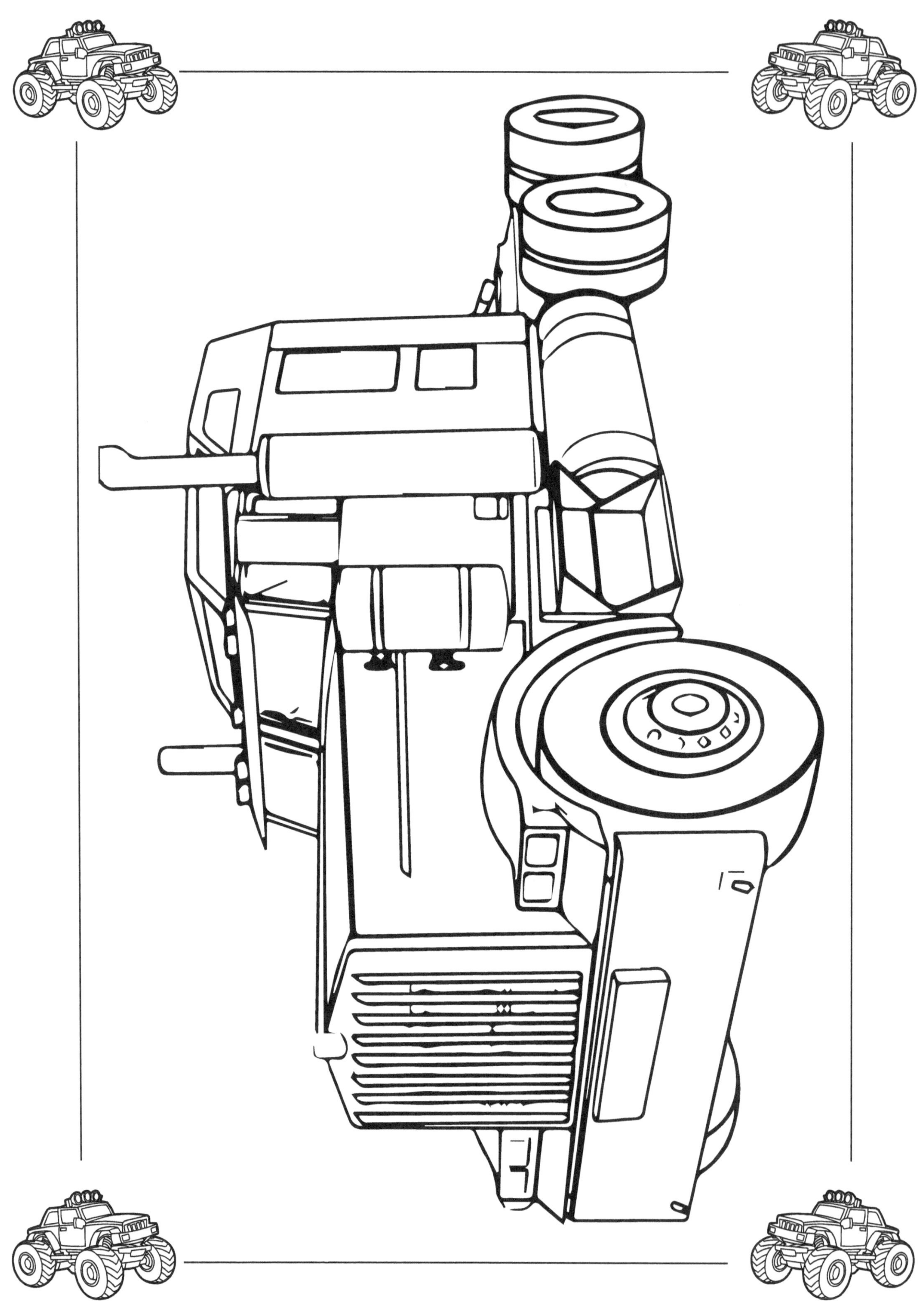

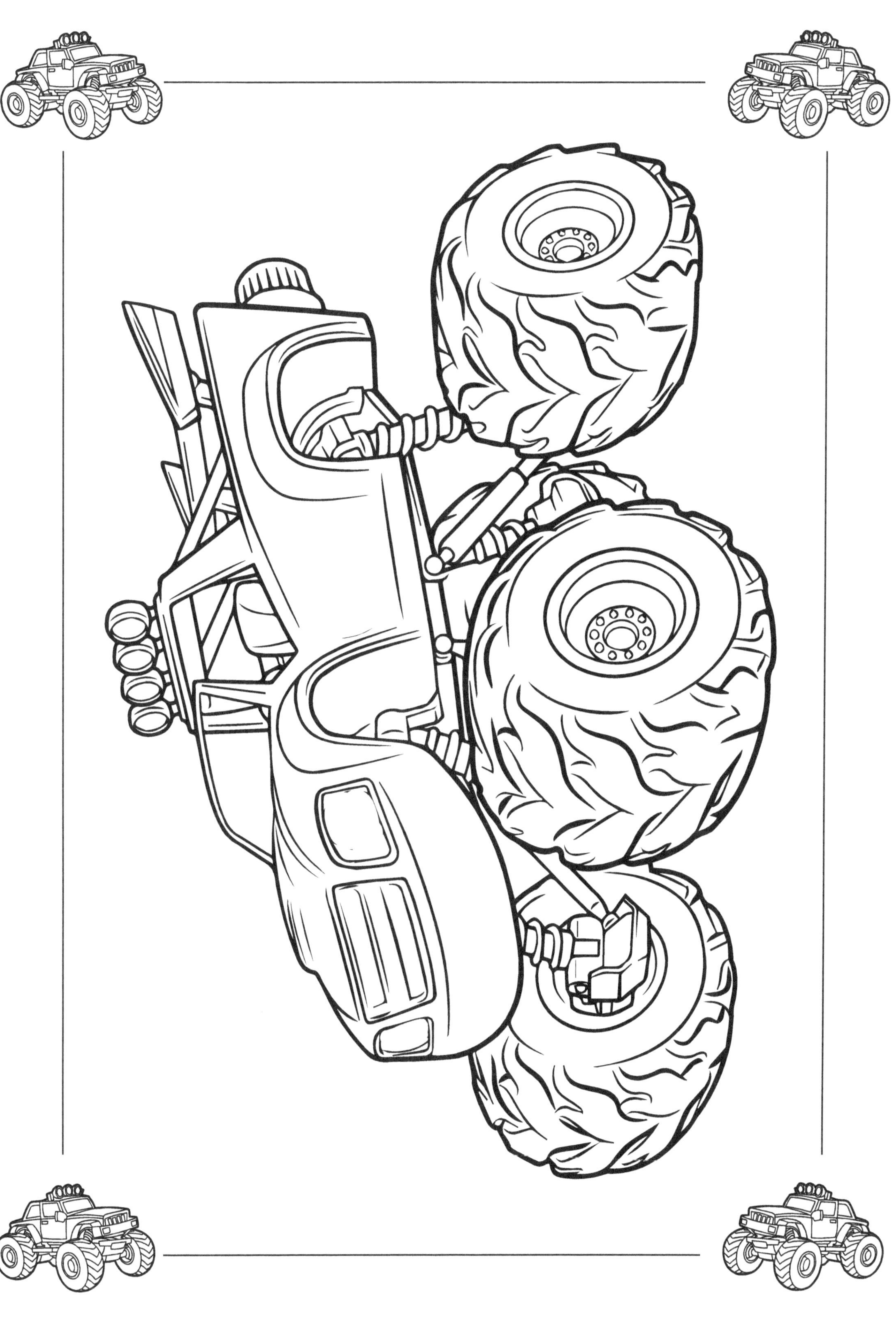

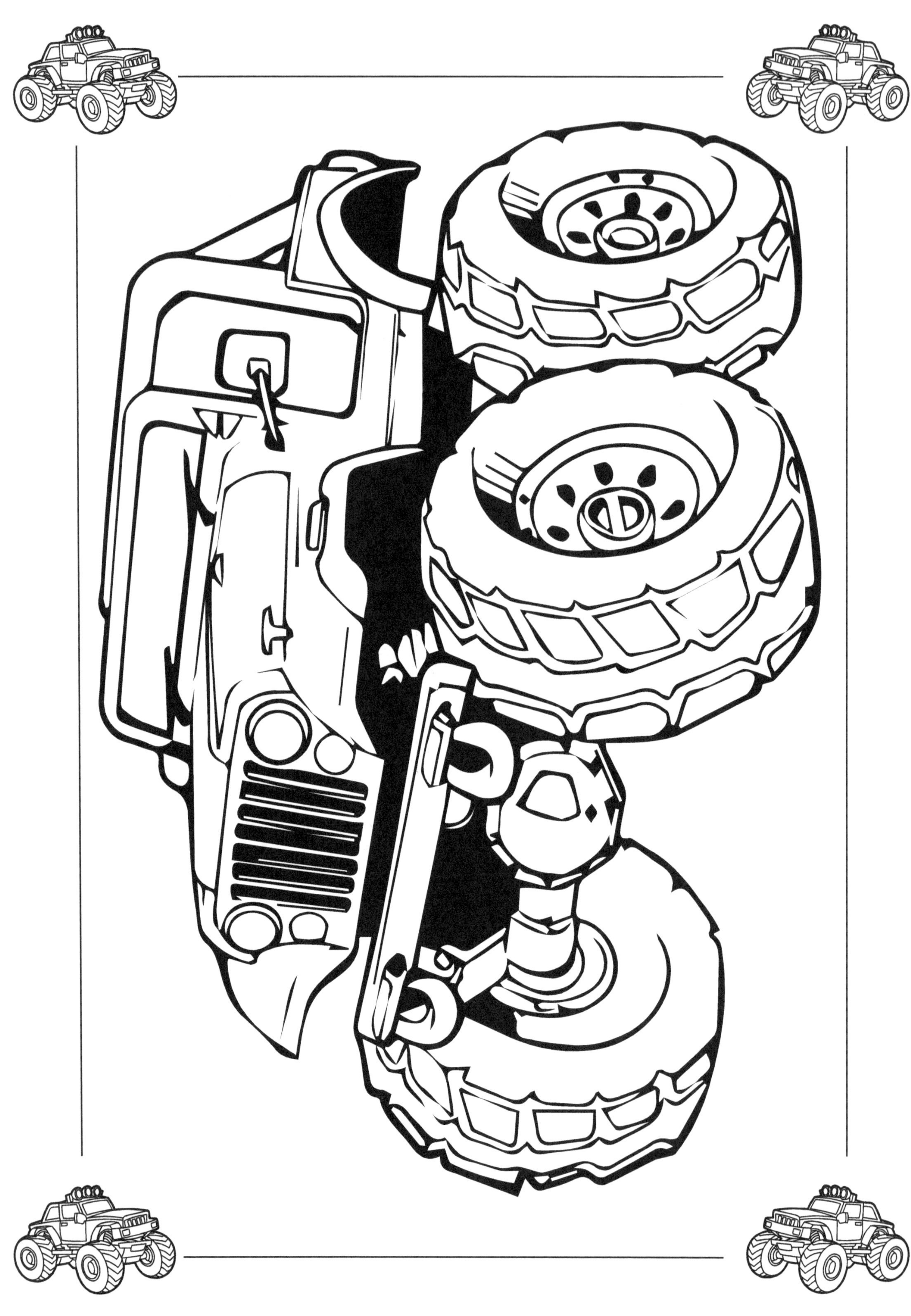

HELP THE MONSTRE

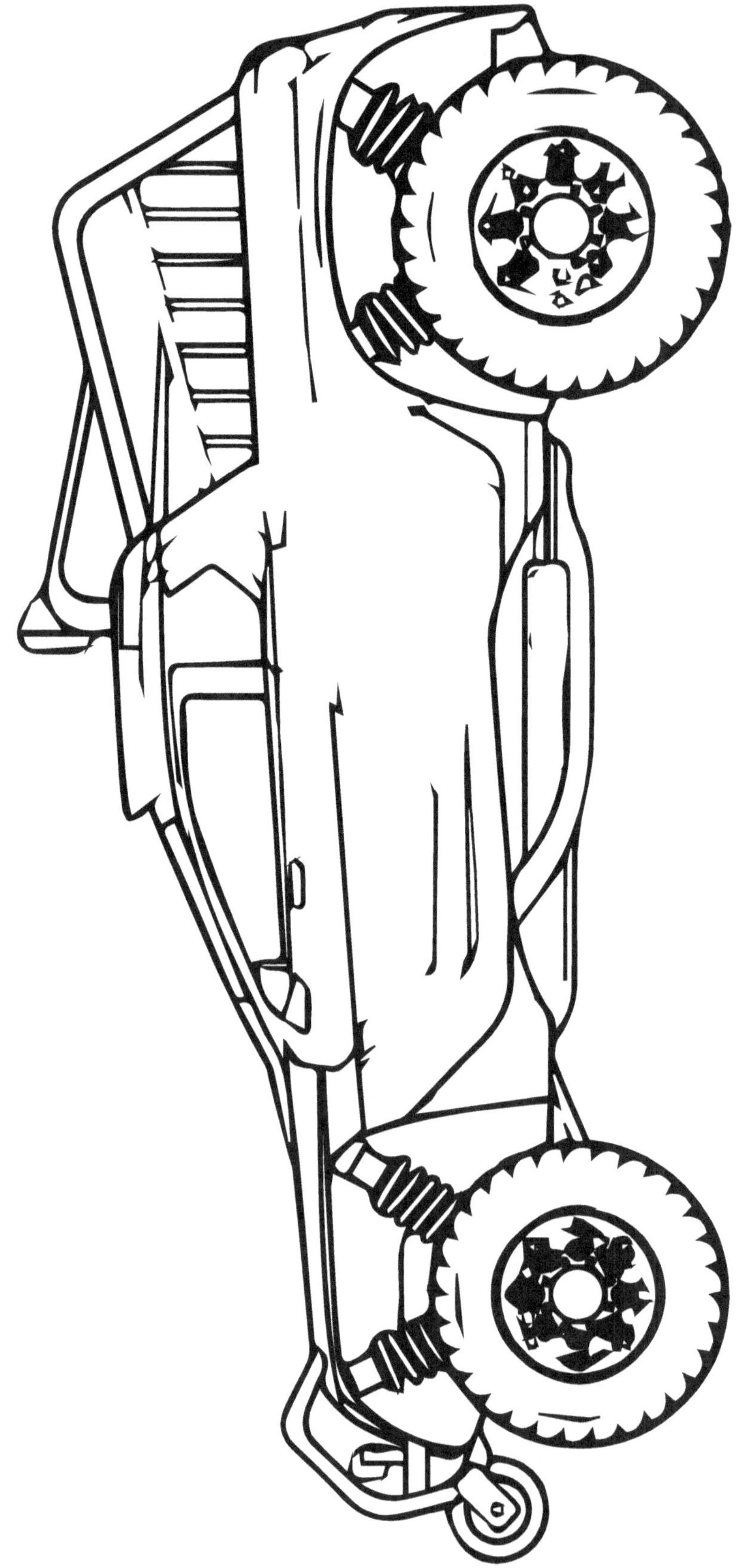

FEED THE MONSTRE

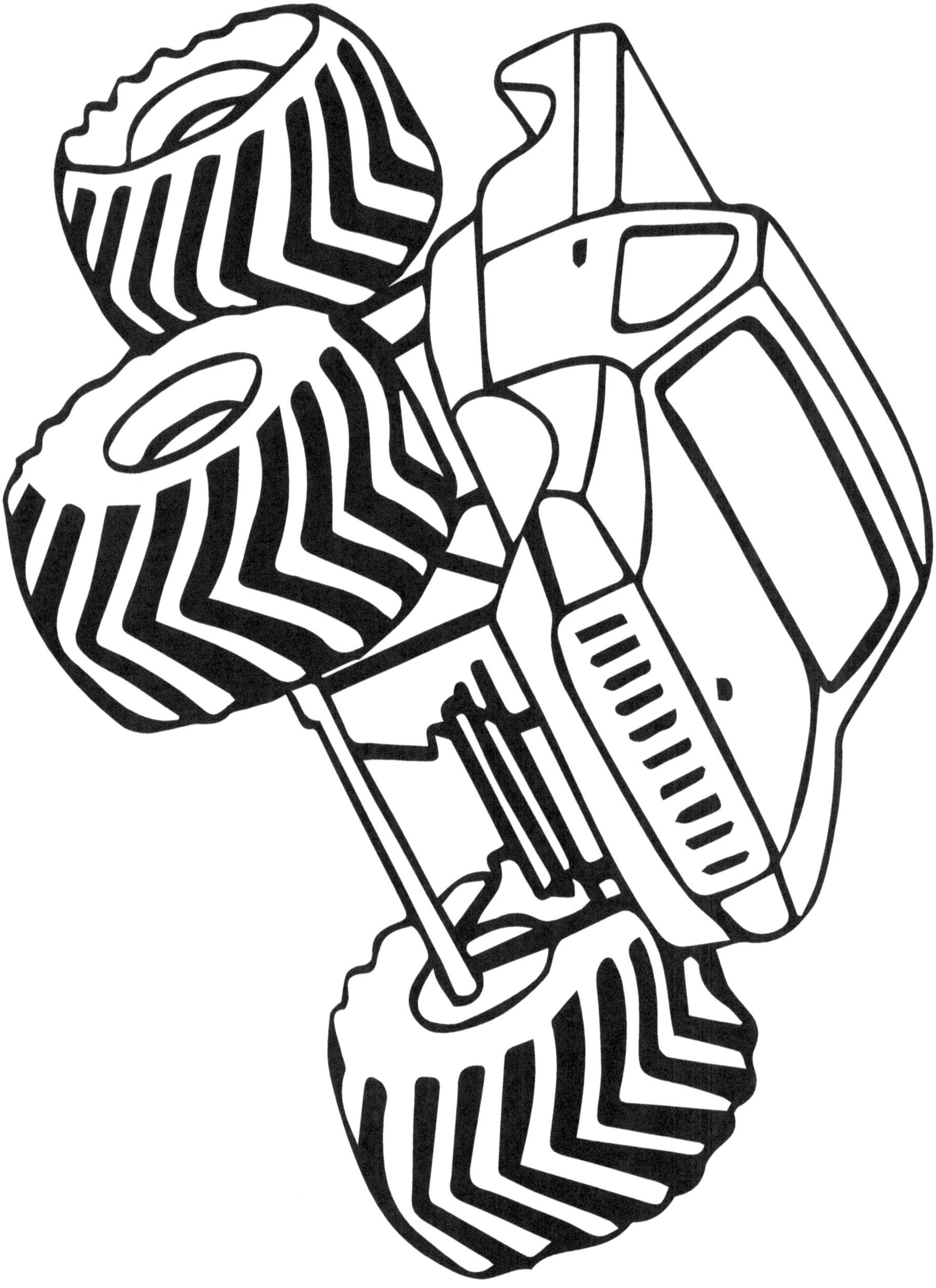

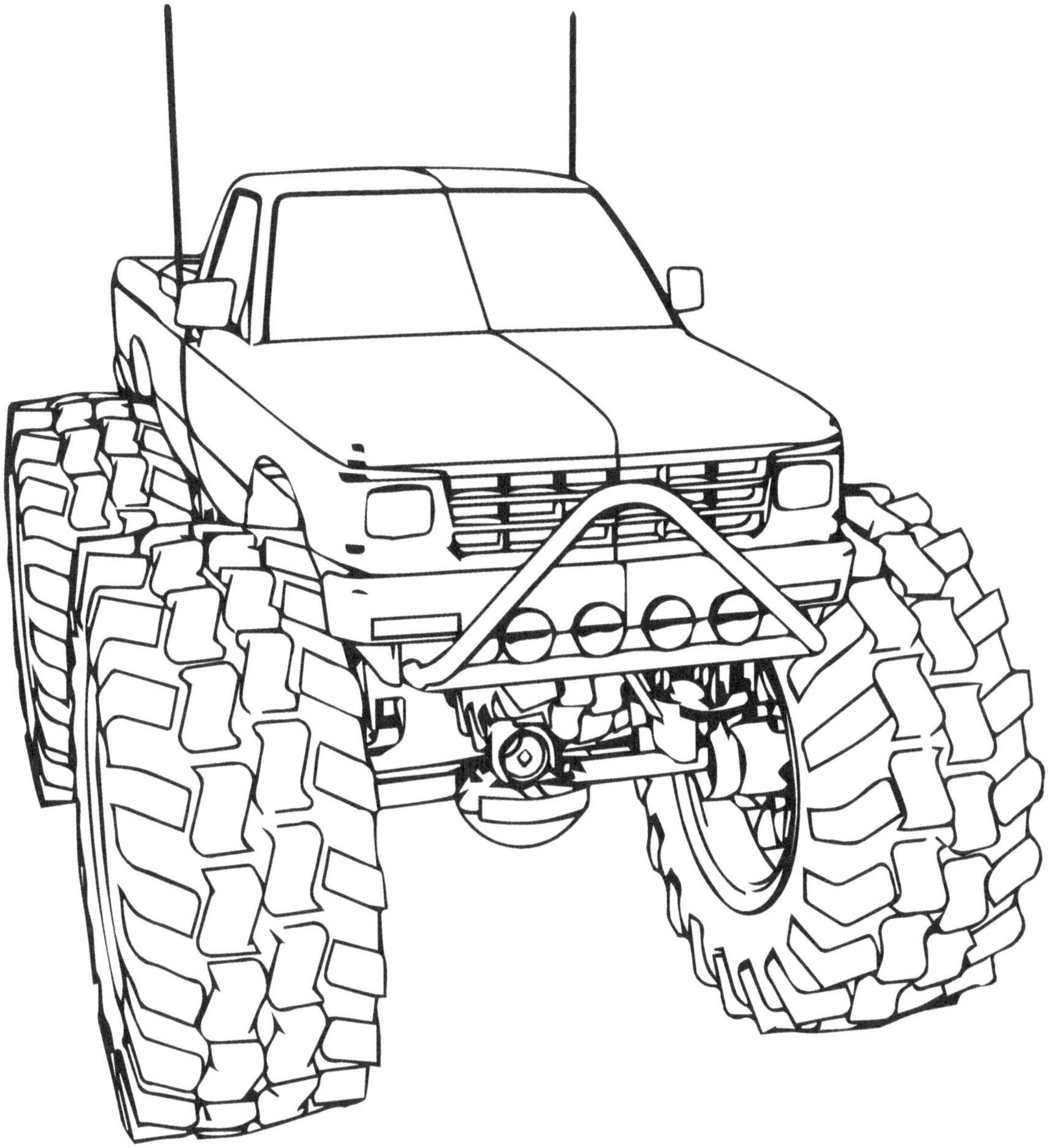

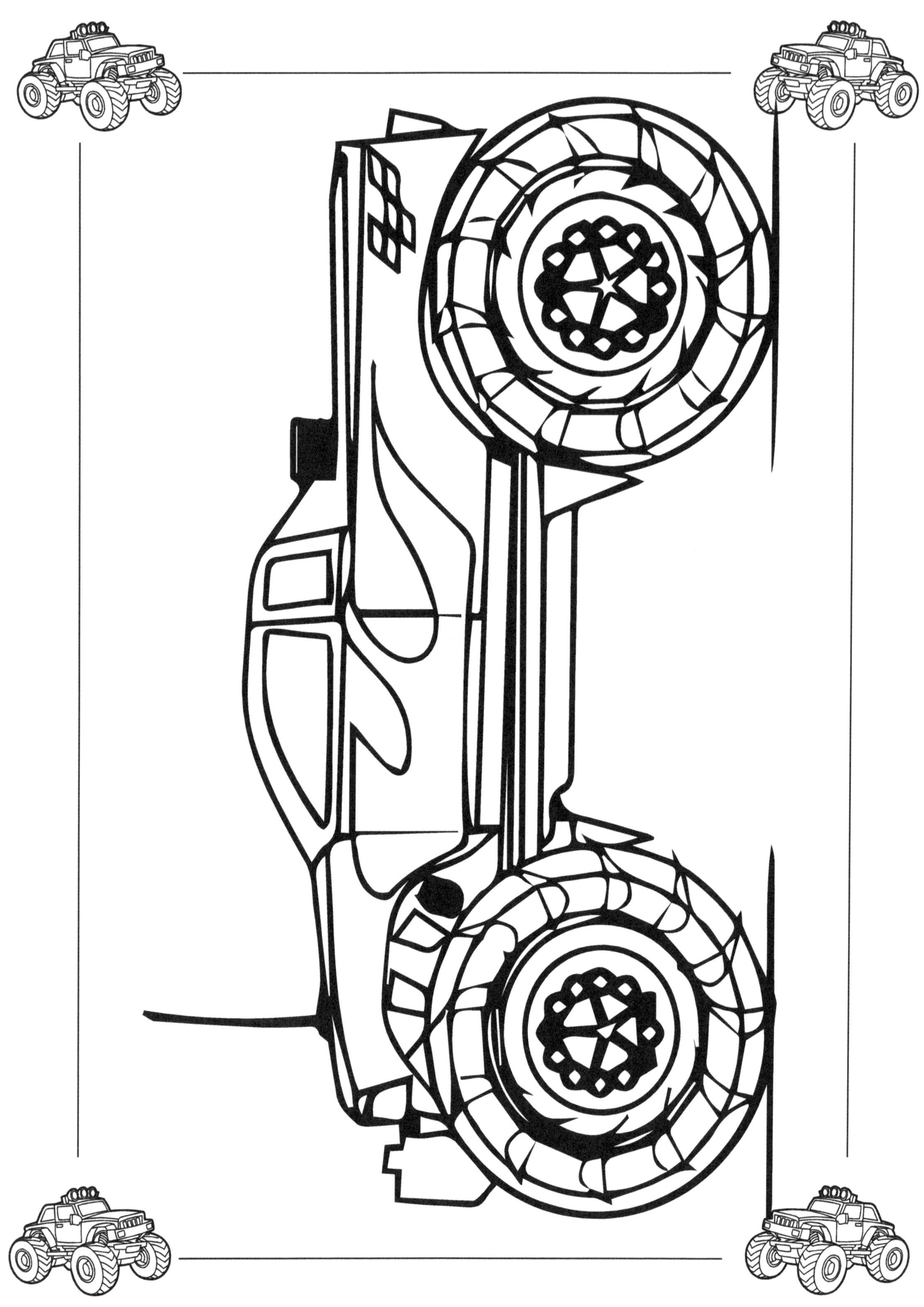

HELP THE MONSTRE

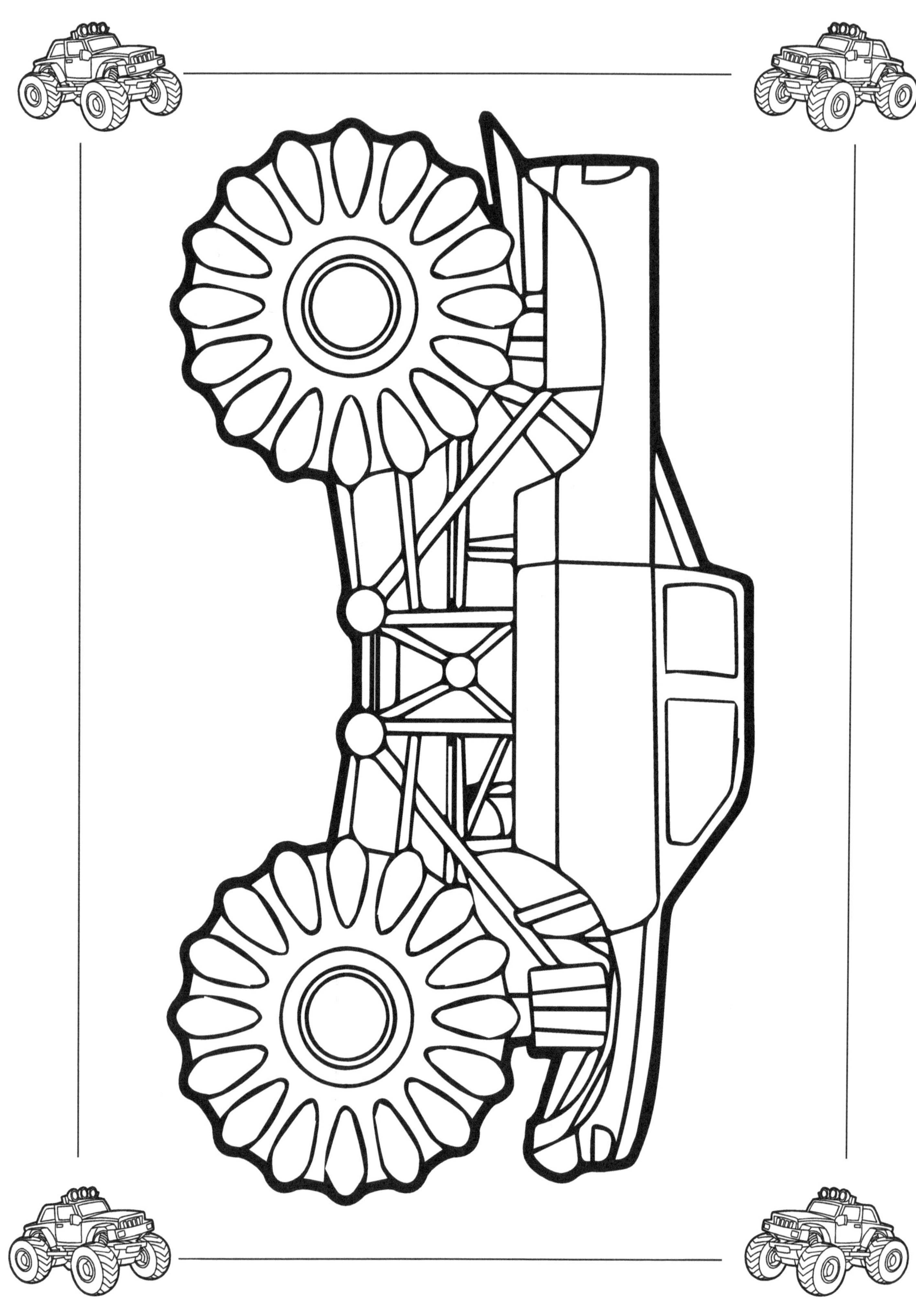

FEED THE MONSTRE

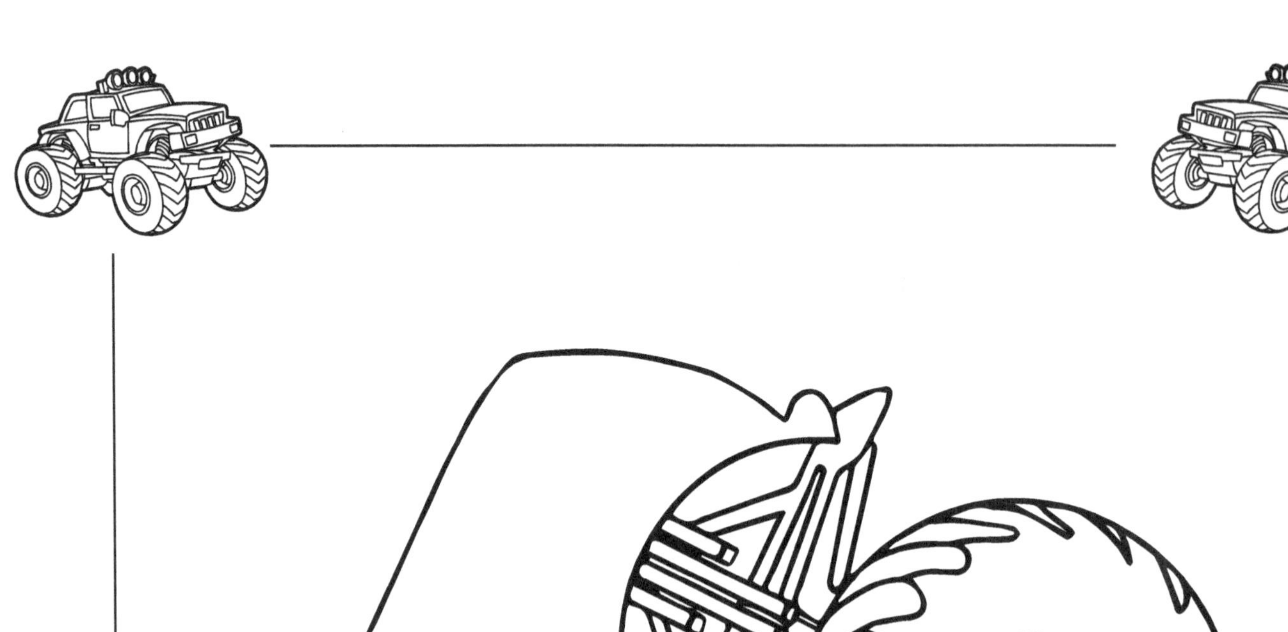

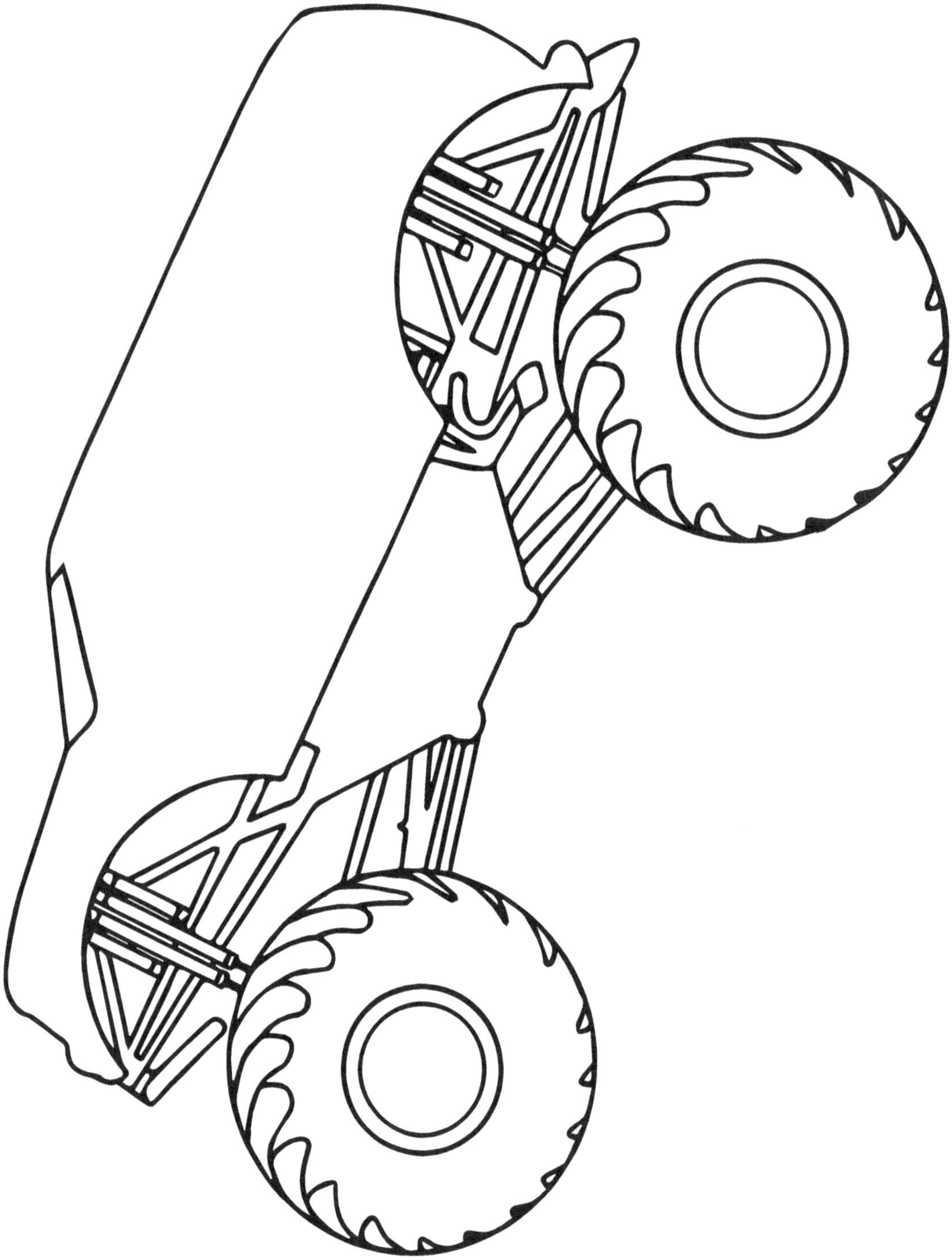

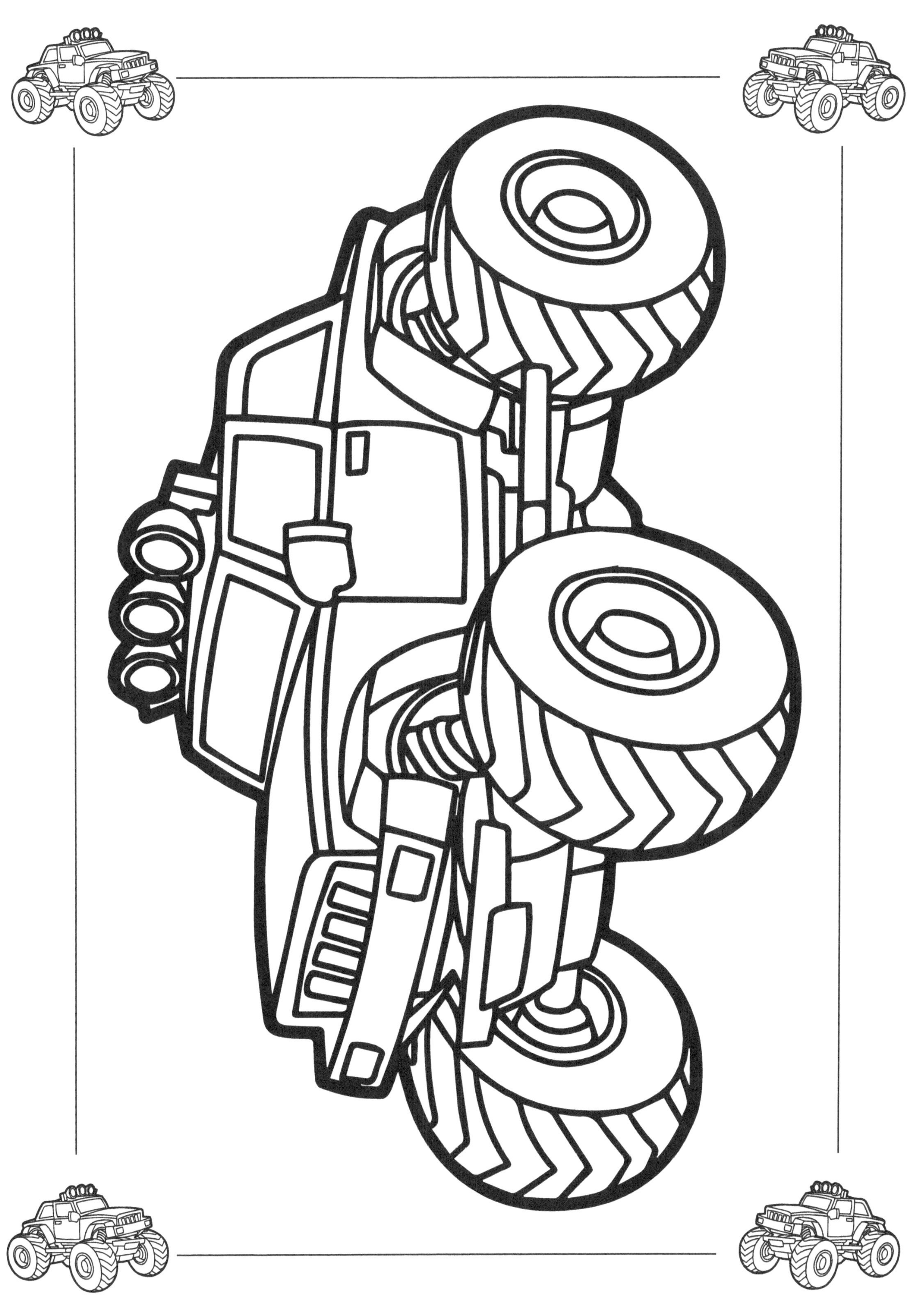

FEED THE MONSTRE

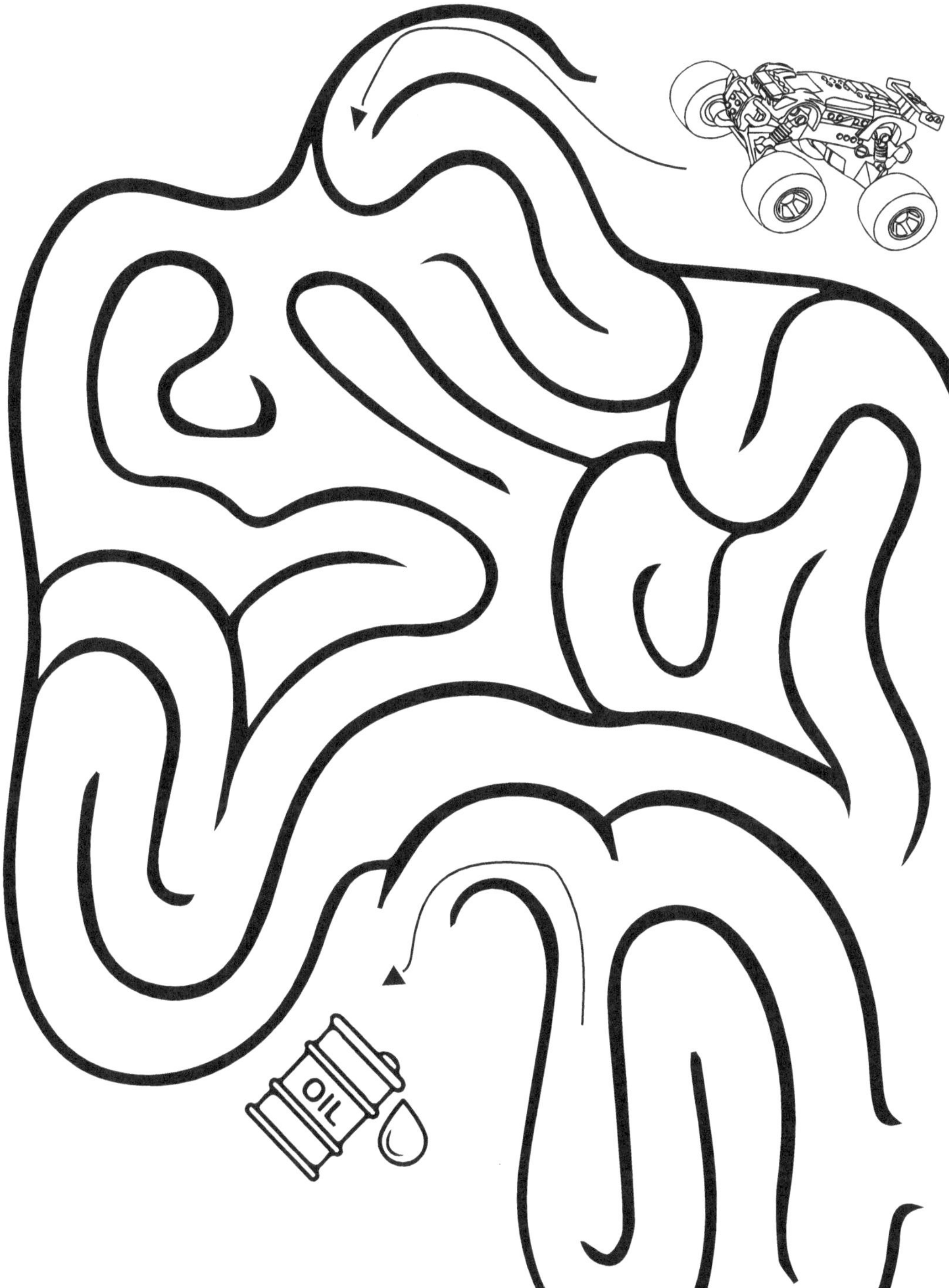

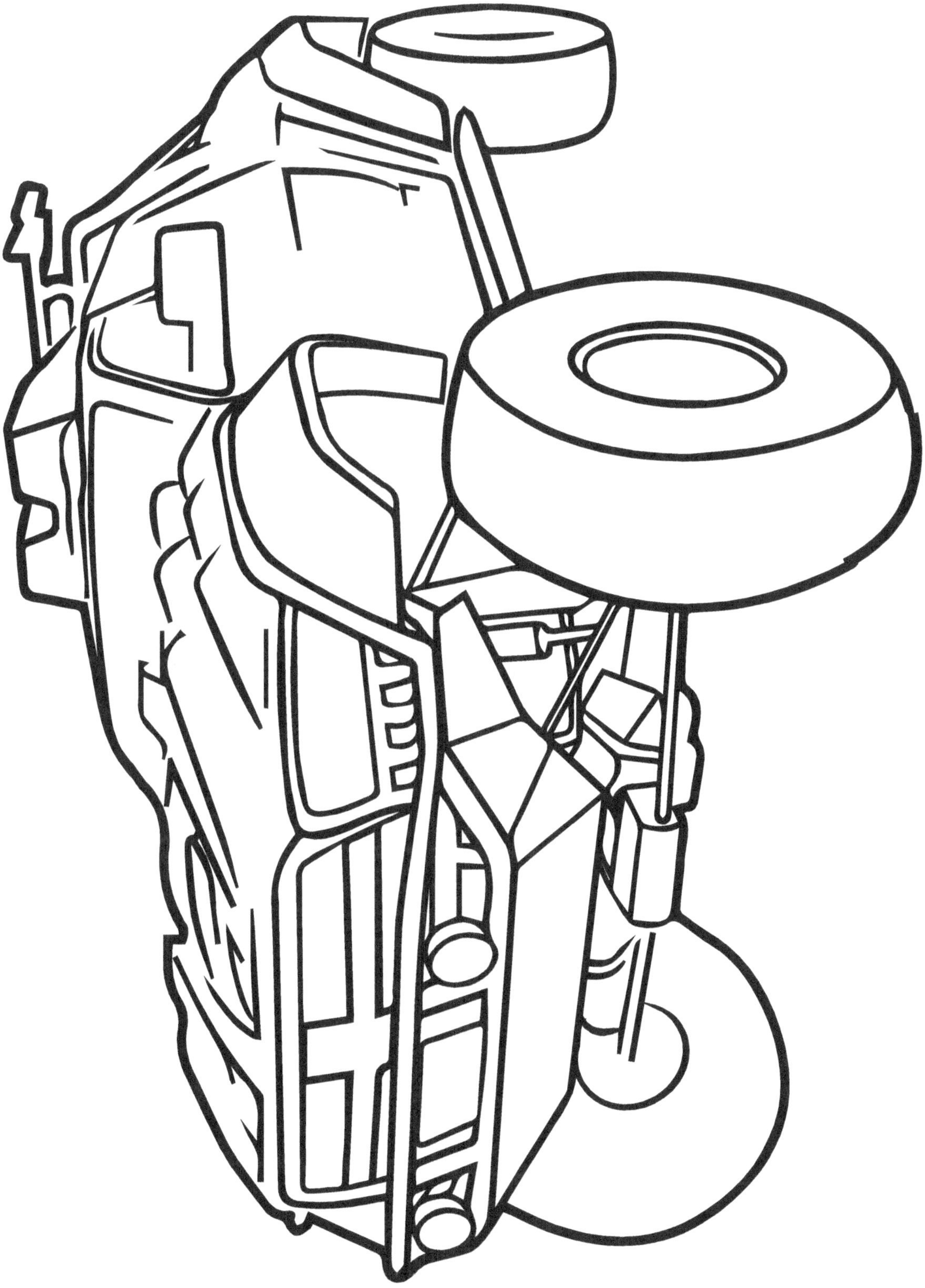

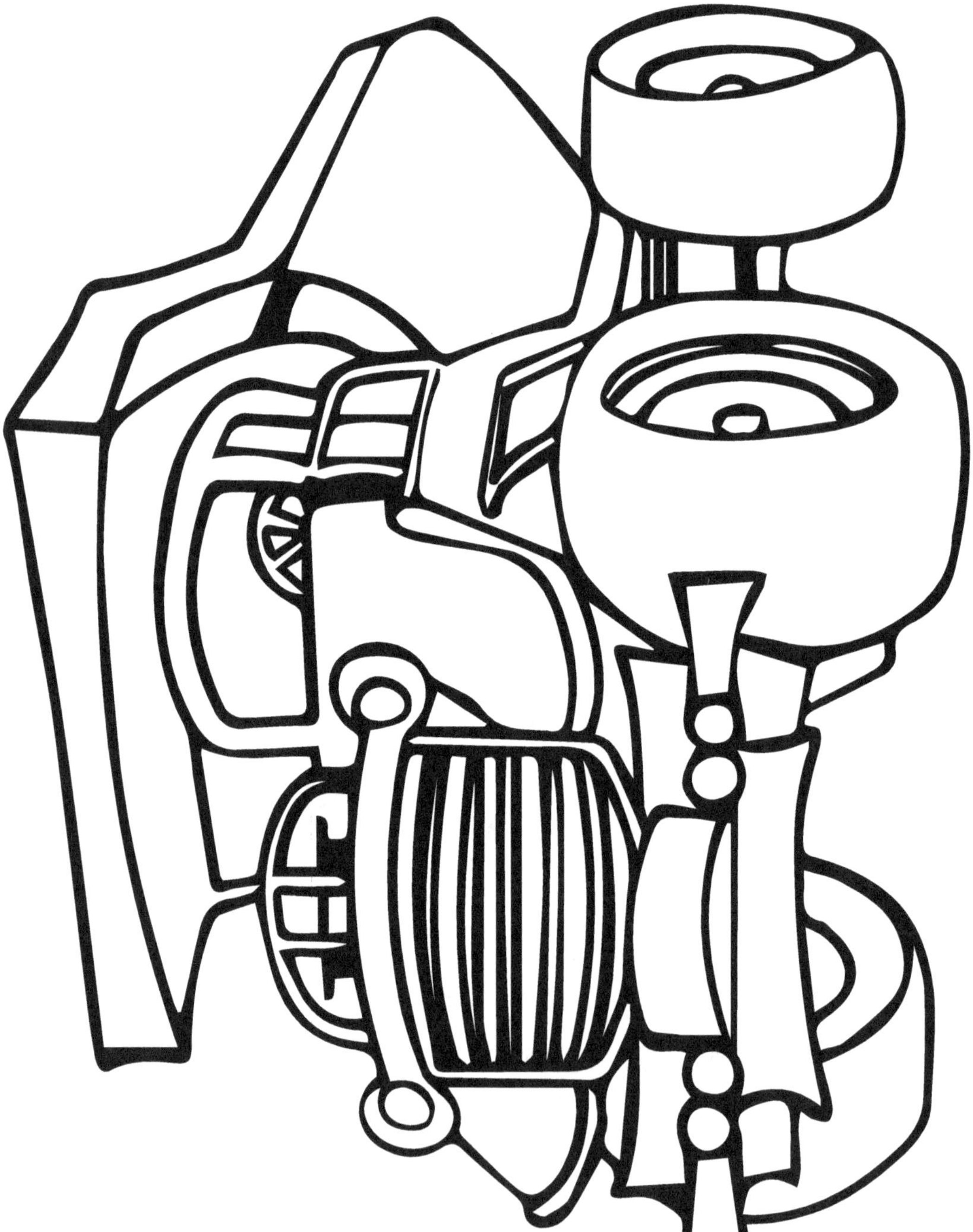

FEED THE MONSTRE

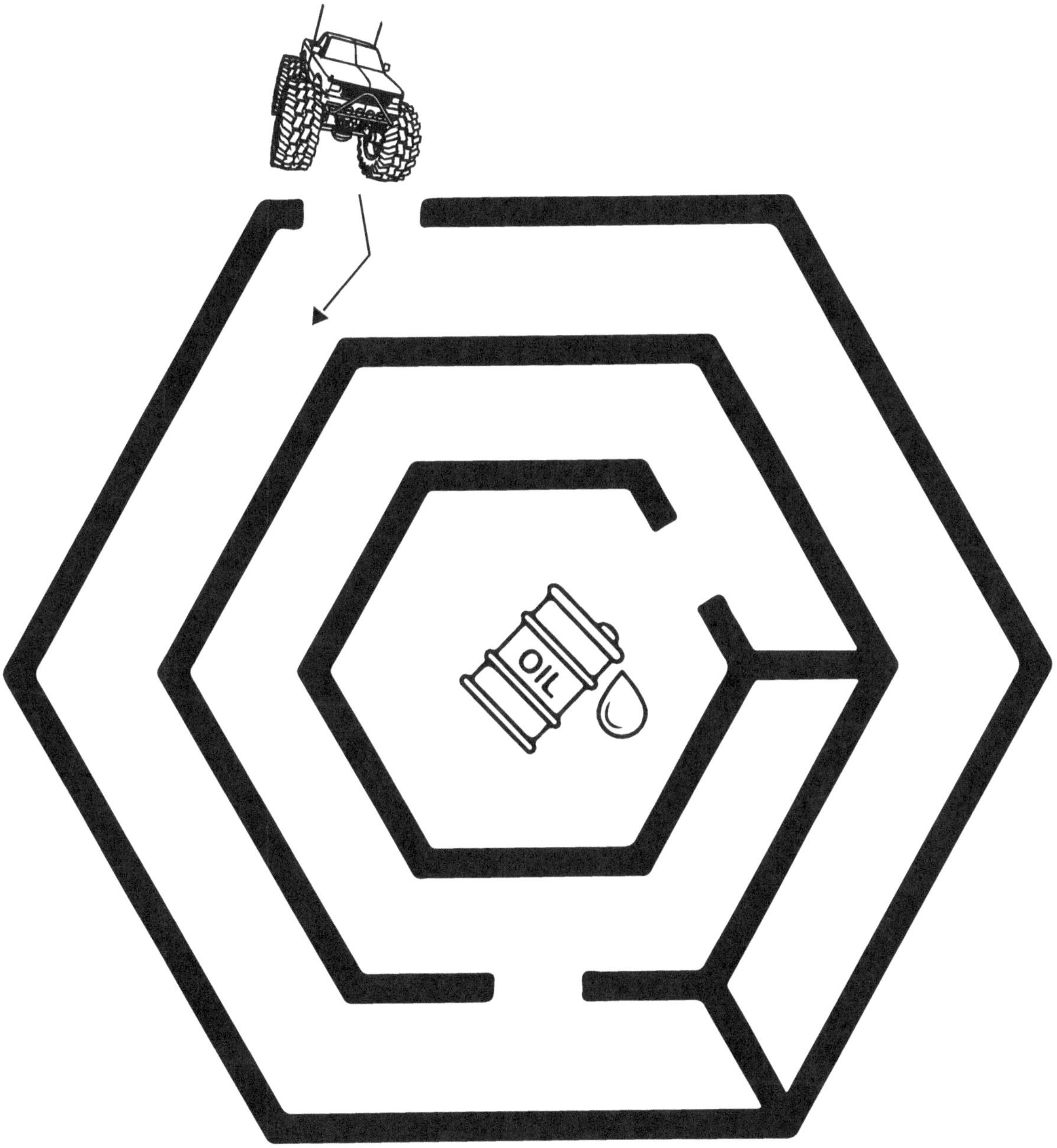

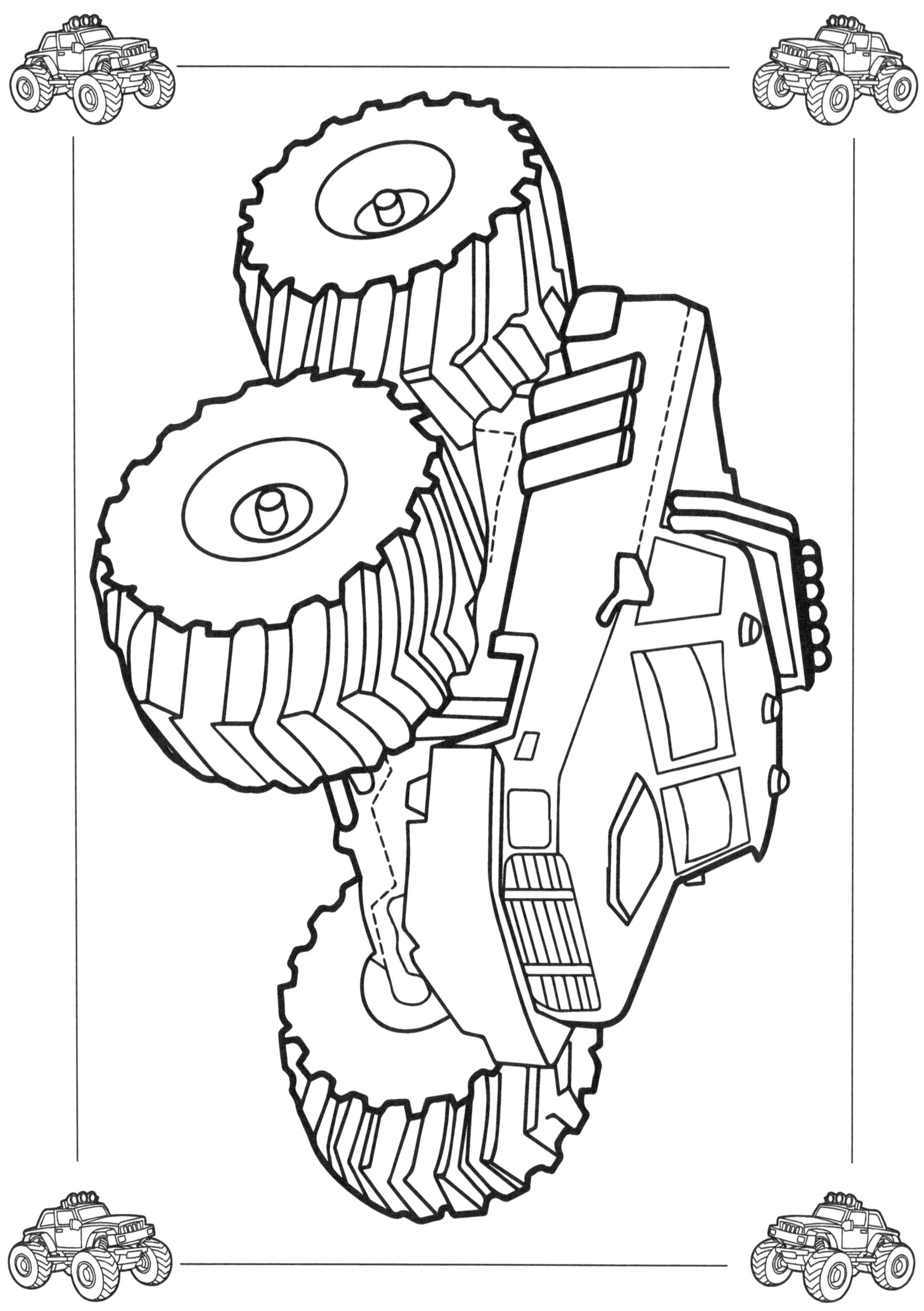

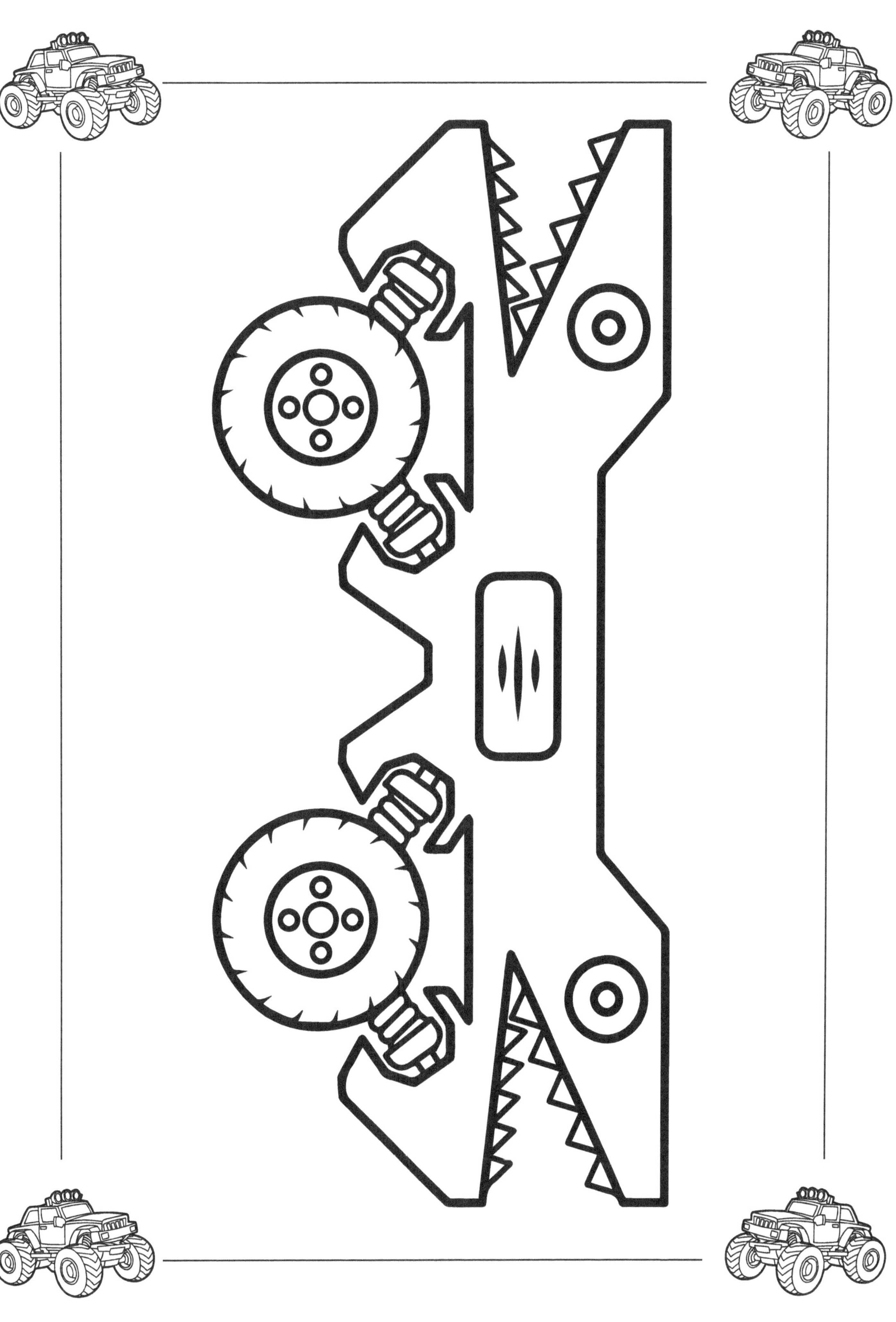

FEED THE MONSTRE

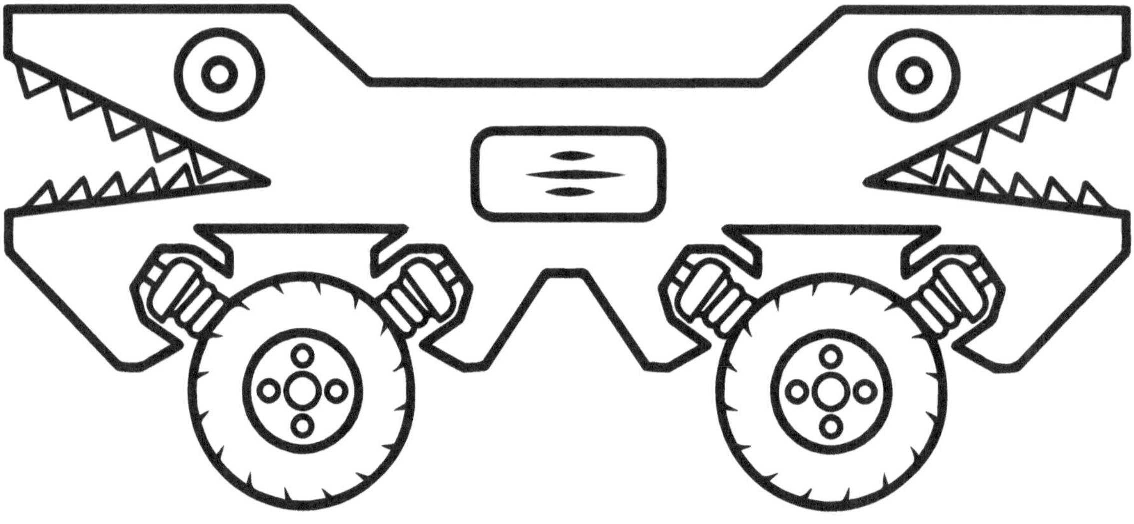

THANK YOU

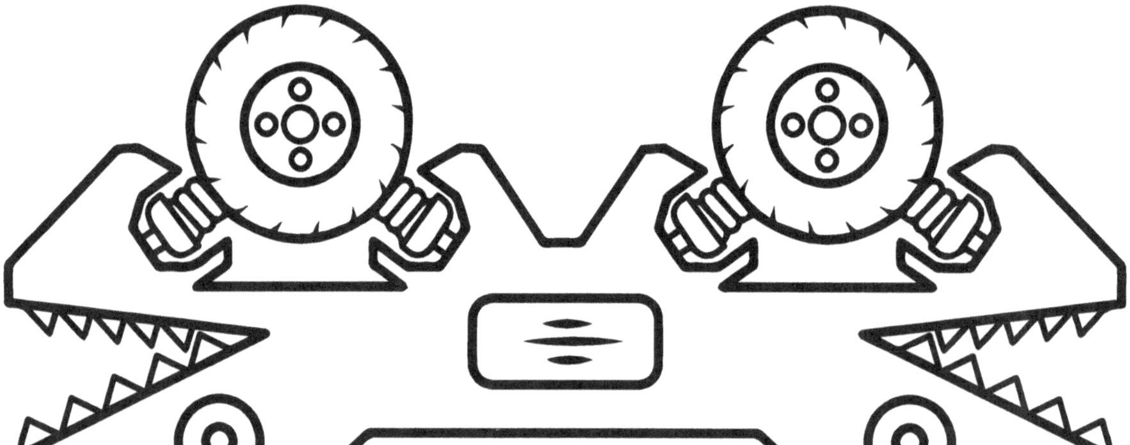

by Rachad